blue

strong

What Is an
ADJECTIVE?

hot

hungry

small

fast

by Jennifer Fandel

Consulting Editor: Gail Saunders-Smith, PhD

PARTS OF SPEECH

CAPSTONE PRESS
a capstone imprint

Pebble Plus is published by Capstone Press,
1710 Roe Crest Drive, North Mankato, Minnesota 56003.
www.capstonepub.com

Library of Congress Cataloging-in-Publication Data
Cataloging-in-publication information is on file with the Library of Congress.
ISBN 978-1-62065-129-2 (library binding)
ISBN 978-1-4765-1738-4 (ebook PDF)

Editorial Credits
Jill Kalz, editor; Heidi Thompson, designer; Marcie Spence, media researcher; Laura Manthe, production specialist

Photo Credits
Capstone Studio: Karon Dubke, 11; Shutterstock: AISPIX by Image Source, 7, Artpose Adam Borkowski, cover (ball), Boris Sosnovyy, 15, Cristi Matei, 9, Dmitriy Shironosov, 19, Knumina, 5, Lenkadan, 13, MarcusVDT, cover (boy), Richard Peterson, cover (rabbit), Rudchenko Lillia, 21, sai0112, cover (strawberry), Zinaida, 17

Note to Parents and Teachers

The Parts of Speech set supports English language arts standards related to grammar. This book describes and illustrates adjectives. The images support early readers in understanding the text. The repetition of words and phrases helps early readers learn new words. This book also introduces early readers to subject-specific vocabulary words, which are defined in the Glossary section. Early readers may need assistance to read some words and to use the Table of Contents, Glossary, Read More, Internet Sites, and Index sections of the book.

Printed in the United States of America in North Mankato, Minnesota.
092012   006933CGS13

Table of Contents

Giving Details

Which one? What kind? How many? An adjective answers these questions. It's one part of speech that gives a detail about something.

orange

cute

soft

eight

5

Adjectives always give

details about nouns.

They make nouns clearer.

Nouns are people, places,

or objects.

blue shirt
adjective noun

hungry boy
adjective noun

hot soup
adjective noun

7

Spotting Adjectives

To find an adjective
in a sentence, first find
a noun. If the word before
the noun gives a detail,
it's an adjective.

The white dog barks.
noun

Being verbs often tie nouns and adjectives together. The words "is" and "are" are being verbs. Find the adjective after the being verb.

The pizza is <u>yummy</u>!

noun

being verb

A noun may have

more than one adjective.

Adjectives are usually joined

with the word "and"

or with commas.

The small and fast pony runs.

The small, fast pony runs.

13

Sentences often have more than one noun. And each noun can have any number of adjectives. More adjectives mean more details.

The <u>blue</u>, <u>green</u>, <u>yellow</u>, <u>orange</u>, and <u>red</u> balloons float into the <u>clear</u> sky.

Same or Different?

Adjectives can show

how two things are different.

These adjectives have "er"

as an ending.

The moon is <u>brighter</u> than the stars.

Adjectives can also show the most or least of three or more things. These adjectives end in "est."

Clara is the __strongest__ girl in her class.

Adjectives tell us
how nouns look, smell,
sound, taste, and feel.
They make the sea blue
and the sand warm.

Glossary

being verb—a word used to express a condition

comma—a punctuation mark used to separate words, groups of words, or numbers

detail—one of many facts about something

noun—a word that names a person, place, or object

object—anything that can be seen and touched; a thing

verb—a word used to express action or condition

Read More

Cleary, Brian P. *Quirky, Jerky, Extra-Perky: More about Adjectives.* Words Are Categorical. Minneapolis: Millbrook Press, 2007.

Dahl, Michael, and Nancy Loewen. *If You Were a Noun, a Verb, an Adjective, an Adverb, a Pronoun, a Conjunction, an Interjection, a Preposition.* Word Fun. Minneapolis: Picture Window Books, 2009.

Internet Sites

FactHound offers a safe, fun way to find Internet sites related to this book. All of the sites on FactHound have been researched by our staff.

Here's all you do:

Visit *www.facthound.com*

Type in this code: 9781620651292

Index

Word Count: 177
Grade: 2
Early-Intervention Level: 21

24